# IN THE
# BEGINNING

D1518153

## God's Story & People in Genesis

© 2022 Lifeway Press®

ISBN 978-1-0877-6744-4
Item 005838149
Dewey Decimal Classification Number: 242
Subject Heading: DEVOTIONAL LITERATURE / BIBLE STUDY AND TEACHING / GOD

Printed in the United States of America.

Student Ministry Publishing
Lifeway Resources
One Lifeway Plaza
Nashville, Tennessee 37234

We believe that the Bible has God for its author; salvation for its end; truth, without any mixture of error, for its matter; and that all Scripture is totally true and trustworthy. To review Lifeway's doctrinal guideline, please visit www.lifeway.com/doctrinalguideline.

# publishing team

*Director, Student Ministry*
Ben Trueblood

*Manager, Student Ministry Publishing*
John Paul Basham

*Editorial Team Leader*
Karen Daniel

*Writer*
Ross Harvey

*Content Editor*
Kyle Wiltshire

*Production Editor*
April-Lyn Caouette

*Graphic Designer*
Shiloh Stufflebeam

# TABLE OF CONTENTS

# INTRO

Almost everyone wants to know how the world began. Scientists, philosophers, and regular people alike have debated the beginning of time since . . . well, the beginning of time. In the book of Genesis, we have the true account of how everything began, from the grandness of the universe to the tiniest atoms that make up the tiniest animals, and everything in-between.

Genesis doesn't just tell the story of the beginning of time. It tells the story of the beginning of you and me, and our relationship with the One who created us. It tells about how we threw that relationship away, and how regardless, the Creator never let us go. It tells about the beginning of the world's problems. It gives glimpses of how those problems will one day be solved. It contains stories of those who didn't know God but were used by Him for purposes they couldn't imagine. Genesis contains stories of betrayal and forgiveness, love and hatred, pain and triumph, banishment and reinstatement; it contains stories that make you laugh and stories that make you weep, as well. Genesis holds invaluable truths that help us know where we come from and what we are called to do with our lives.

The book of Genesis has it all. Most importantly, since it is God's Word to us, it has the power to change our lives. If we give God our time and attention as we examine this book, He will strengthen our faith and understanding of His nature and character. Genesis is the beginning, and by the end of the next thirty days, my prayer for you is that you see God more clearly and love Him more deeply through the reading of His Word. Like the characters in this true story, we are imperfect people who often stubbornly try to do things our own way and figure things out on our own. However, if we can learn to trust God's plan for our lives and believe in Him as our King, we will find great peace, joy, and encouragement through the book of Genesis.

# GETTING STARTED

*This devotional contains thirty days of content, broken down into sections. Each day is divided into three elements—**discover, delight, and display**—to help you grow in your faith.*

## discover

This section helps you examine the passage in light of who God is and determine what it says about your identity in relationship to Him. Included here is the daily Scripture reading and key verses, along with illustrations and commentary to guide you as you learn more about God's Word.

## delight

In this section, you'll be challenged by questions and activities that help you see how God is alive and active in every detail of His Word and your life.

## display

Here's where you take action. This section calls you to apply what you've learned through each day.

**Each day also includes a prayer activity at the conclusion of the devotion.**

Throughout the devotional, you'll also find extra items to help you connect with the topic personally, such as Scripture memory verses, additional resources, and interactive articles.

# CREATION

# TO

# THE

# TOWER OF BABYLON

God created everything, and it was perfect—that is, until humans got involved. To say that humankind got off to a shaky start is putting it lightly. However, through each mistake and poor decision, God revealed His love and mercy— and the proof that despite what it may have looked like, He has everything under control.

# DAY 1

# NAME, IMAGE, LIKENESS

## discover

READ GENESIS 1.

**So God created man in his own image; he created him in
the image of God; he created them male and female.
—Genesis 1:27**

In the beginning, God created the heavens and the earth. Whether it's the striking colors as the fall leaves change, or the warm rays of the sun when you step outside on a spring afternoon, you don't have to look far to recognize the beauty of God's creation. Yet, God says that the most beautiful thing He created is us—humans. The day and night, sun and moon, plants and animals—all were good, and God was pleased when He spoke them into existence. But when God formed us from the dust of the ground, He said it was *very* good.

In part, God was so pleased because we are made in His likeness. Man and woman—male and female—were created as image bearers of God. As a picture shows the details of whatever it captures, we were made to show the world around us the very nature of who God is. Of course, just like a photograph isn't the real thing, we are not God; we are God's representatives, the best of His creation. God uniquely gave us purpose and responsibility to take care of creation, fill the earth, and rule over it. Since we were made to show God's character, all we had to do was obey God to accurately show the world who He is! You probably know how that turned out. Soon, what was once very good would be thrown into chaos.

# delight

**Review what God created on each of the first five days. What do you learn about God's character when you think about everything He created?**

**In what ways do humans differ from the other things God created?**

**As you live your life, how can you show the world what God is like?**

# display

Find a printed photograph of yourself, or print a photograph of yourself, and place it somewhere you will see it every day, such as a bathroom mirror or a refrigerator door. Place a note next to the photo that says, "Made in the image of God." Just as that photograph is your image, you bear the image of God. You were made with incredible purpose, identity, and responsibility. You have the capability to show the world the glory of the one, true God. How will you live for God's glory today?

God, please help me to live for Your glory each day. Show me what it means to be made in Your image. Thank You for how You've made me, and how You love me even when I don't represent You as well as I could. Please guide me as I seek to grow in my knowledge and trust of You through the study of Your Word. Amen.

## DAY 2

# FAILURE BUT HOPE

## discover

READ GENESIS 3.

**"I will put hostility between you and the woman, and
between your offspring and her offspring. He will
strike your head, and you will strike his heel."
—Genesis 3:15**

When you make a mistake, your immediate next action is probably to gauge the consequences of that mistake. If you drop your phone, you check to see if the screen is cracked. If you back your car into a pole, you see if there is a dent in your bumper. If you run straight into your friend in the hallway, you check to see if they are okay. When Adam and Eve sinned in the garden, they would have realized their sin changed things, but they wouldn't have been able to comprehend the horrific and tragic consequences of their disobedience to God. The world around them went from perfect to broken in an instant. They went from walking and talking with God to being separated from Him. Everything negative about the world around us is a result of what happened in Genesis 3.

Thankfully, God doesn't operate the same way we do. He doesn't need to look for the consequences of our sin, because He isn't surprised by our actions or their results. Rather, He is always working for the good of those who love Him (see Rom. 8:28), even when our actions go against His desires. That same truth was evident in Adam and Eve's lives. Even though God knew Adam and Eve's choice would set His perfect creation into chaos, God immediately promised them (and us) that He would eventually redeem the effects of sin, defeat the enemy that offers humanity a counterfeit version of God's design, and bring everything back to a perfect state. In spite of our imperfection, God offers hope.

# delight

**Think about a choice you've made recently that wasn't the best. How did the consequences affect you?**

**How did the consequences affect others?**

**Read 1 John 1:9-10. What does God say we should do when we sin?**

# display

Think about the last person who was affected by a sinful choice you made. It could be a sibling, a friend, or even someone you struggle to get along with. Pray for courage, and then approach that person and have a conversation with them. Confess what you did wrong, and ask for their forgiveness. Write down the result of this conversation, and make note of how it felt after you confessed what you did wrong.

God, thank You for making a plan to save us from the effects and punishment of sin. Thank You for loving me even when I mess up. Help me to rely on You as I work to make the choices You want me to make. Amen.

In The Beginning

# SNOWBALL

## discover

READ GENESIS 4:1-16.

**Then the Lord said to Cain, "Why are you furious? And why do you look despondent? If you do what is right, won't you be accepted? But if you do not do what is right, sin is crouching at the door. Its desire is for you, but you must rule over it." —Genesis 4:6-7**

As a kid, I loved snowball fights. Once, I tried to make an enormous snowball in hopes of conquering my heavily-bundled rivals. The key to making a large snowball is getting the ball big enough so that you can roll it along the snow easily, so it rapidly picks up more snow as you roll it.

Sin works a lot like that snowball rolling in the snow. If sin continues to live in our hearts and actions, it will grow out of control before we even realize it. In Genesis 4, it had only been one generation since the first-ever sin, and that sin was already causing problems. Cain, Adam and Eve's first son, would let the sin of greed, jealousy, and pride spiral into something far worse. When he didn't bring his best offering to God, he became angry at the favor God showed to his brother Abel and Abel's offering. God even warned Cain that sin was "crouching at his door." But he didn't listen. Cain got his brother alone, and then attacked his brother and murdered him.

Sin is dangerous because, at the very core of it, it is us saying we know better than God. We only go our own way because we don't trust God or His guidelines for our lives. We decide we know best, and we mess everything up in the process. Thankfully, God offers us freedom from sin: if anyone trusts in Jesus, they are free from the punishment of sin and sin's control over their lives.

# delight

**God told Cain that sin was "crouching at the door." It was waiting to attack Cain. What needs to happen in your heart and mind for you to see sin as something out to get you rather than something enticing?**

**Have you ever noticed one particular sin leading to other sin in your life? If so, write down the sin you struggle with that starts the snowball effect for you, and pray for the strength to rule over it.**

# display

If left unchecked, sin can continue down a vicious cycle that only leads to destruction (see Ps. 1:6). To stop the cycle, we must repent: acknowledge the sin in our lives and turn to God for freedom from it. It's best if we do it as quickly as possible—before the snowball keeps rolling and becomes bigger than we ever imagined. If you wrote down a sin from your own life in answer to the previous question, repent and talk to God today (and if needed, speak to a parent or trusted adult about what you are struggling with and how to overcome it).

**God, I realize sin has a destructive effect on my life. Please help me recognize sin in my own life, and help me turn away from it. Thank You for giving me the power to walk away from sin through Jesus's life, death, and resurrection. Thank You for giving me the gift of forgiveness. Amen.**

# DAY 4

# I'M DIFFERENT

## discover

READ GENESIS 6:5-22.

**These are the family records of Noah. Noah was a righteous man,
blameless among his contemporaries; Noah walked with God.
—Genesis 6:9**

By the time of Noah, sin had become so widespread that God was
exasperated with His creation. The world was filled with evil. It had
gotten so bad God said He "regretted that he made" humanity
(see Gen. 6:6). Yikes.

In the middle of the bad was some good. Well, one good. His name was
Noah. The Bible said he was a righteous man, one who walked with God.
Despite the disobedience around Him, Noah stayed close to God and
followed God instead of those around him. Because of this, Noah would
survive the coming flood. In it, everything would be destroyed—that
is, everything except for Noah, his family, and enough of the animals to
repopulate the earth afterward.

If you look around today, you'll notice that people are still up to their
evil, selfish deeds. Look even closer, and you'll see in your own life how
your sinful decisions can cause all kinds of destruction. Noah walked with
God, and because of that, his life was spared. Noah wasn't perfect, but
he reminds us that it will go much better for us when we are walking
with, spending time with, and cherishing our relationship with God over
everything else. Like Noah, be different in your time, and put God first; you
may be surprised how it changes your life.

# delight

**What gets in the way of you spending consistent time with God (i.e., reading His Word, praying to Him, etc.)?**

**What was different about Noah? Do you live differently than the people around you who don't follow God? Why or why not?**

# display

Pull out whatever you use to keep your schedule or calendar, or use the alarm on your phone. Set a reminder for a consistent time this week to spend reading God's Word and doing this devotion. If you are already consistently spending time with God, awesome! Keep after it and grow in your relationship with Him.

**God, thank You for being patient with us, even though we still do things that break Your heart. Thank You for reminding me that it's okay to be different, as long as I put You first. Help me to put You first each day, and help me to spend time with You each day. Amen.**

## DAY 5

# ONE DOOR CLOSES, AND . . .

## discover

READ GENESIS 7.

**Those that entered, male and female of every creature, entered
just as God had commanded him. Then the LORD shut him in.
—Genesis 7:16**

Trusting God can be difficult, especially when we can't see exactly what will happen afterward. However, trusting God is always the right thing to do. God commanded Noah to build a giant boat—an ark—for his family and all of the animals to board and escape the coming flood. Noah trusted God in this, despite never having seen a flood that big before. Noah built the ark, the animals arrived, and they all boarded—seven days before the skies opened up and the rain didn't stop for forty days.

When they entered the ark, something interesting happened. The Bible says God shut them in (see Gen. 7:16). God made a way for Noah's safety and provided the final act in shutting the ark with Noah, his family, and the animals safely inside. Noah obeyed God, but it was God who chose to protect and save Noah and his family.

The account of the ark points us to Jesus and what He did for us. We obey God because we trust Him, but ultimately it's Jesus who saves us by His life, death, and resurrection; salvation isn't anything we could ever earn on our own. Just as God saved Noah from the flood, God saves us from eternal separation from Him because He loves us. God closed the door for Noah so that Noah could rest safely inside. God defeated sin and death and achieved victory for us when Jesus breathed again. When the tomb opened up, it opened the way for us to come into relationship and be safe with Him. One door closed and one door opened: and in both, it was God that provided the miraculous action. Because of that, we, like Noah, can be saved.

# delight

**How does it make you feel to know that God has opened the door and invited you into relationship with Him?**

**Who do you know who needs to know about God? Write their names below.**

# display

Make a post on social media that says, "God invites us in!" Maybe you can add a picture of a door or an ark. If you don't have social media, make those words the background on your phone or write them on the outside of a notebook or binder. If someone asks you about your post or those words, explain to them how the story of Noah points to the story of Jesus.

God, I am glad that Your rescue plan for us is all about what Jesus did. I praise You because we can rely on Your power and not our own. Help me share Your story with others, and help me trust You to give me the courage to do so. Amen.

# DAY 6

# UNCONDITIONAL

## discover

READ GENESIS 8.

When the LORD smelled the pleasing aroma, he said to himself, "I will never again curse the ground because of human beings, even though the inclination of the human heart is evil from youth onward. And I will never again strike down every living thing as I have done."
—Genesis 8:21

As humans, we sometimes have a hard time understanding certain aspects of God. Maybe it's because our language can't perfectly describe an indescribable God, or maybe it's because God is eternal and we live bound by time. One of those things that many people have trouble grasping is God's unconditional love. No matter what, God loves us. Even as God's displeasure with the sin that had gone wild in the world grew and He decided to flood the earth, God loved us enough that He gave us another chance. Through Noah, the world would continue to exist and people would continue to live in it. God also made a promise: no matter what else happened—no matter what evil humans did, what mistakes we made, how far we strayed from God—He would never again destroy the Earth by flood.

It's amazing to think that God knows the contents of our heart and mind, but loves us anyway. He loves us like a perfect Father loves His children. Even when we choose to go against Him and go our own way, God loves us. He loves us enough to promise that He would never wipe us out again, and He loves us so much that He sent His one and only Son to die in our place. It is an incredible encouragement, comfort, and cause for joy that God will always love us, no matter what.

# delight

**What in your life reminds you of God's love for you? Write down as many reminders as possible.**

**Which verses in the Bible remind you of God's love? Write down three Bible verses below and highlight them in your Bible or Bible app.**

# display

Find a worship song that helps remind you of God's love for you. Put it in your music rotation, and listen to it at least once each day for a week (ask your parent's permission before making any internet purchases).

**God, thank You for Your unconditional love. Thank You for Your promises to us, and thank You for being faithful and never changing. Help me to remember Your love for me when I feel unloved, and help me to remember what You did through Jesus when I need Your peace and joy. Amen.**

And God said, "This is the sign of the covenant I am making between me and you and every living creature with you, a covenant for all future generations: I have placed my bow in the clouds, and it will be a sign of the covenant between me and the earth."

—Genesis 9:12-13

# BETTER THAN A PINKY PROMISE

## discover

READ GENESIS 9:1-17.

**And God said, "This is the sign of the covenant I am making between me and you and every living creature with you, a covenant for all future generations: I have placed my bow in the clouds, and it will be a sign of the covenant between me and the earth."**
**—Genesis 9:12-13**

Being able to trust someone is a great feeling. When you know that you can depend on them, no matter what, you have great confidence in your relationship with them. This could be a feeling you have with a best friend, a sibling, or a parent. As much as we can trust other people who we are close to, we can trust God even more! When God made the promise to Noah that He would never again flood the world, He was doing more than making a promise—He was making a covenant. A covenant is an agreement that goes beyond our definition of a promise. A covenant is more like a contract, containing defined consequences if broken. However, when God made this agreement, He put no requirements on Noah. God only put requirements on Himself—only He was required to follow through with what He promised.

Imagine making a deal with someone where you were the only one who had something to lose! It doesn't quite make sense to us. But God, in making the covenant with Noah—and with all of creation—was showing that sacrificial love is what He is all about. God is willing to give up Himself just for us. In this act, God was most focused on demonstrating how much He cares for us. We see evidence of this truth throughout the Bible, and it's one of the reasons we know we can trust God, no matter what.

# delight

**As you reflect on the story of Noah, what reminders of God's love do you see?**

**Read 1 John 4:7-19. What about love stands out to you as significant from this passage?**

# display

God showed His love by making a covenant with us—a promise for which only God needed to keep the requirements. How can you go out of your way to show God's love to someone else this week? In the space below, make a plan and follow through this week.

**God, thank You for once again demonstrating Your love for us. Thank You for how You love us, even when we don't deserve it and when we go back on our word to You and others. Help us to be more like You in how we love others and keep our word to others. Amen.**

# DAY 8

# OUT OF ORDER

## discover

READ GENESIS 11:1-9.

**"Come, let's go down there and confuse their language so
that they will not understand one another's speech."
—Genesis 11:7**

One Christmas, I received a full-sized outdoor basketball hoop to place in my driveway. In my excitedness, I immediately went outside and began to put it together. Having seen basketball hoops before, I figured I could do it without consulting the instruction manual. As you may have guessed, this resulted in a whole day of frustration. By the end of Christmas day, I was no closer to shooting hoops than when I had begun.

Those who made the hoop created instructions so that I would understand how to assemble it properly. They were the experts (having designed the hoop) and it would have been wise for me to pay attention to them. But I believed I didn't need help and that I could do it by myself. My perspective was out of order.

In Genesis 11, humans had once again forgotten about God. They decided to get together and build a tower that reached the heavens; in doing so, they believed they would have the power and fame of God. However, God knew better. He knew humanity would continue to grow in their pride and arrogance and would destroy themselves if they didn't change. So God scattered the people around the Earth and confused their language so that they could not continue to try to do everything on their own. This is a reminder to us, as well: we must remember that God is God—He is the Leader and we are the followers. Our perspective is out of order if we ever think that we know it all.

# delight

**What happens when we try to do things meant for God to do (e.g., make decisions without waiting for Him to guide us, try to do good deeds to earn forgiveness, try to fight temptation on our own, etc.)?**

**In which areas of your life do you need to be patient and wait for God's direction and guidance?**

# display

If we say that God is our God, we need to allow Him to be the one who leads our lives. We should lean on Him for our decisions each and every day. Identify some areas of your life where you tend to act before first talking to God. Write down those problem spots somewhere that will catch your attention, and try to remember to let God be your God in those areas in the future.

**God, thank You for being the one true God, whose power is unlimited. Because You are God, I can trust You in every area of my life, and I don't ever have to do anything by myself. Thank You for promising to always be there for me. Help me to remember to rely on You each day. Amen.**

# ABRAHAM, SARAH,

## AND

# ISAAC

Abraham, a man who didn't even know God, would be used to bless the entire world. His story is a reminder that God has a perfect purpose for each of us. When we submit to God, He does amazing things.

## DAY 9

# RING, RING

## discover

READ GENESIS 12.

**The LORD appeared to Abram and said, "To your offspring I will give this land." So he built an altar there to the LORD who had appeared to him.**
**—Genesis 12:7**

Can you believe there was once a time on earth before contact lists and caller ID? When your phone rang, you just picked it up and relied on the person on the other end of the line to introduce themselves. Today, we almost always know exactly who is calling every time our phone rings. When we don't recognize the number, we usually don't answer the phone.

In Genesis 12, the story of one of the most important men in history begins, the story of a man named Abram. Unlike Noah, Abram didn't follow God. He had no relationship with God. He didn't even know God! However, God wanted to use him to change the world. God called Abram; that is, He spoke to Abram and explained that He wanted Abram to believe in Him. God told Abram He had a purpose and a plan for his life. He would make Abram's children into a great nation. Abram answered the call, and obeyed!

Even though Abram didn't know God at the time, he left his family, friends, and homeland and headed toward the land God would show him. Interestingly, Canaan (the Promised Land) wasn't empty when Abram arrived, but he still believed God would give the land over to him when the time was right. Despite this invitation probably looking highly skeptical to Abram's human eyes, Abram decided to trust God and His words over what he could understand by his own comprehension.

# delight

**What would it take for you to pick up everything you own and move to an unknown location?**

**Read Proverbs 3:5-6. How do these verses encourage you to trust God even when you don't understand everything about His plan?**

# display

In order for Abram to trust God and His plan, he had to be willing to let go of the things he held close. Abram didn't know the plan, so he had to be willing to follow God step by step. What desires or possessions do you hold on to that you are unwilling to give over to God? Write them down on a sheet of paper and pray over them. When you are ready, crumple the paper up and throw it in the trash, signifying that you won't let anything hold you back from following God's plan for your life.

God, thank You for loving me so much that You have a specific, unique plan for my life. If there is anything in my life I am unwilling to give up for You, please show me what it is. Help my desire be to follow You first and foremost. When You call me to what is next, help me answer You and follow with full confidence. Amen.

# DAY 10

# IN GOOD COMPANY

## discover

READ GENESIS 14:17-22.

> "...and blessed be God Most High who has
> handed over your enemies to you."
> And Abram gave him a tenth of everything.
> —Genesis 14:20

Have you ever met someone so unique that your encounter with them is ingrained in your memory? On his journey around the land that would eventually belong to God's people, Abram met many people. One of the most interesting people he met was a man named Melchizedek. While Abram was returning from a battle against armies that had captured his nephew, Lot, Melchizedek met Abram and blessed him—not simply because Abram had won the battle, but because Melchizedek knew that God was with Abram. Melchizedek also blessed God, for it was God who defeated Abram's enemies.

The story of Abram and Melchizedek ends there. What makes this encounter so interesting? Melchizedek was the king of Salem and a priest of the one true God. Who else was both a priest—a representative of the people who spoke to God for them—and a king—the anointed leader of the people? Jesus, too, holds both of those titles. In Hebrews 7:2, the author writes that "Abraham gave Melchizedek a tenth of everything. First, his name means king of righteousness, then also, king of Salem, meaning king of peace." We know little about where Melchizedek came from, or really, much else about him, but the author says he "[resembles] the Son of God; he remains a priest forever." Melchizedek is a foreshadowing, a hint of what is to come in Jesus. In Jesus we find righteousness and peace, perfectly. He is our priest eternally. This encounter is not only a sneak peek to the future but a reminder to us that God's plan is perfect in every way.

In The Beginning

# delight

**Read Hebrews 7. What sticks out to you in this chapter?**

**What other examples of the foreshadowing of Jesus have we seen so far in the book of Genesis?**

# display

Jesus is both our King and Priest, even though we probably more often think about Jesus as King than we think about His priestly nature. The High Priest spoke to God for the people. Because Jesus died and rose again, we have direct access to God. In heaven, Jesus sits next to God, speaking to Him on our behalf. He is our High Priest forever. Imagine if we had to talk to a pastor every time we needed to communicate with God! Thank God He made a way for you to speak to Him directly! Take some time to write down some of the characteristics of Jesus that you find in Hebrews 7 and in other places in Scripture.

God, thank You for showing us the beauty of Jesus through the Old Testament. Thank You for using Abram and Melchizedek, and for showing us that You design beautiful stories for Your people. Thank You for making a way that we could speak directly to You. Help us to always honor Jesus the way we should. Amen.

In The Beginning

# FAITH IS BELIEVING

## discover

READ GENESIS 15.

He took him outside and said, "Look at the sky and count the stars, if you are able to count them." Then he said to him, "Your offspring will be that numerous." Abram believed the Lord, and he credited it to him as righteousness.
—Genesis 15:5-6

God is a God of promises. When God says something, He means it and will follow through. All throughout the Bible, we see God making promises to His people. Oftentimes, God made promises to people when it was hard for them to see those promises come true. They had a choice of whether to believe God or not. God made one of these promises to Abram, telling him he would be the father of a great nation, and that his descendants would be as numerous as the stars in the sky. One problem: Abram had no children. With his human mind, it would have been hard for Abram to see God's promise coming true. However, Abram believed God. Because of his faith, God saw Abram as righteous.

God made us a promise, as well. God promised that He would make a way for us to be forgiven of our sins. When we look at our lives, sometimes that's hard to believe. We make the same mistakes over and over again, and that gives us doubts. In those moments, we need to have faith that God tells the truth. Because of our trust in Jesus and His death on the cross, God credits us with righteousness, as well. Trusting God often means putting aside our human eyes and asking God to see as He sees—and that requires faith like Abram's.

# delight

**What does it mean to be righteous?**

**According to these verses, how do we receive righteousness?**

**How do you show those around you that you have faith in God?**

# display

If you have trusted in Jesus as your Savior and Lord, you have Jesus's righteousness (His perfection) covering you. When God sees you, He sees the perfection of Jesus. That frees us from the shame that Satan tries to place on us when we mess up and sin. Sin is still something we battle against every day, but know that if you are in Christ, God does not hold your sin against you. Remember that truth as you walk with God today. In the space below, write out a sentence or two describing how you feel when you consider that you are covered in the righteousness of Jesus.

**God, thank You for always keeping Your promises. Thank You for forgiving me of my sins and calling me righteous. Please help me to battle against sin in my life today. Help me to live in the freedom You made possible through Jesus. Amen.**

## DAY 12

# I DID IT MY WAY

## discover

READ GENESIS 16.

**So Abram's wife, Sarai, took Hagar, her Egyptian slave, and gave
her to her husband, Abram, as a wife for him. This happened
after Abram had lived in the land of Canaan ten years.
—Genesis 16:3**

I strongly dislike riding in the car with a driver who doesn't use GPS when driving in unfamiliar locations. Personally, I use GPS almost everywhere I go. I prefer to arrive where I need to go on time! However, some people prefer to rely on their own natural sense of direction when they're navigating the road.

In life, you may find that some people are excited to do things their own way, despite advice or experience that says they should do otherwise. In Genesis 16, Abram's wife, Sarai, tried to do things her own way. God had promised her and Abram a son, but up until that point she had been unable to have children. Sarai figured that Abram would only receive a son if it were through another woman, so she gave Abram her maid Hagar as a wife. This was not God's plan; the son they had was not the son God promised. In trying to fulfill God's promise in her own way, Sarai made a huge mess—bringing heartbreak, not blessing.

We often try to find our own way through tough times, situations we don't understand, or experiences we don't want to deal with. Going our own way may seem to work for a short amount of time, but doing things God's way will always be what is best for us. It may mean waiting patiently for God to act instead of taking matters into our own hands, but relying on God is always better than doing it our own way.

In The Beginning

# delight

**What was a time you tried to do things your own way and ended up making a bigger mess?**

**What are some of the reasons we try to make shortcuts in our own life?**

# display

Print a map of directions from your house to your church, or to a church you've gone to before. At the top of that page, write, "God's directions are the correct directions." Place the map in your Bible as a bookmark. Use this as a reminder that we get lost without God. We all need a reminder at times in our lives!

**God, thank You for providing the direction for my life. Please help me to remain patient and wait for Your timing. Lord, You know what I want, and You know what I need. Thank You for always taking care of me, and please help me to remember that when I need it most. Amen.**

# DAY 13

# WHAT'S IN A NAME?

## discover

READ GENESIS 17:1-22.

**"Your name will no longer be Abram; your name will be Abraham, for I will make you the father of many nations."**
**—Genesis 17:5**

Do you know what your name means? Growing up, I remember having a small keepsake on my dresser. It spelled out my first, middle, and last names, and underneath it, the meaning behind those names. Although the meaning behind our names doesn't necessarily determine what we become, it can be a cool reminder of who we are or where we have come from.

In the Bible, we should pay special attention any time God calls someone by a new name. That change of name indicates a change in direction, calling, or purpose. In Genesis 17, God calls Abram and Sarai by new names: Abraham and Sarah, meaning "Father of Many" and "Princess," respectively. Although Abraham and Sarah weren't perfect people, God honored His promise to them and chose to use them in powerful ways. By giving them new identities, God showed the new purpose that He was giving them. God gives us new identities, too. After we trust in Him, He calls us sons and daughters—new identities that show our purpose as His representatives here on Earth.

# delight

**Many names mean aspirational things like "blessed" or "champion." If you had to choose a name for yourself based on your life to this point, what would your name be? What would you want your name to be moving forward?**

**To you, what does it mean to be a son or daughter of God?**

# display

As a son or daughter of God, your calling is to represent Him here on earth. Create two lists in the columns below. On the left, make a list of ways that you represent God well. On the right, make a list of areas of your life where you are still working on representing God well.

| Representing God Well | Still Needs Work |
| --- | --- |
| | |

God, thank You for calling me by a new name. Thank You for making me a member of Your family. Please give me the strength to represent You well wherever I go. Thank You for choosing to use me in a powerful way. Amen.

# FAST FORWARD

## discover

READ GENESIS 18:1-15; 21:1-7.

**The LORD came to Sarah as he had said, and the
LORD did for Sarah what he had promised.
—Genesis 21:1**

As a child, I read a story called "The Magic Thread." The story is about a young boy who wants time to pass more quickly. As he has this thought, a shadowy figure appears and offers the boy a magic ball of thread. The ball of thread is the sum of his days, his life. If he unravels the thread, his life moves forward at a faster pace. If he leaves it alone, his life proceeds at a normal rate (I won't spoil the fable in case you want to read it).

The idea of the story is that we all want time to speed up. We want to know what comes next, or how our story will progress. The truth is, only God knows the entirety of our story. When God told Sarah that she would have a child, she laughed. She couldn't believe that her story would include a child, due to her old age. However, God had made her a promise, and He always keeps His promises. When her son was finally born, she named him Isaac, which means "laughter."

As followers of Jesus, we do best when we remember to trust God with everything we have: our past, present, and future. We may want to see how our story will progress, but we can rest knowing that our promise-keeping God is the One who writes it.

# delight

**Have you ever wanted to life to move faster or skip forward? If so, why?**

**What promises of God do you hold on to when you need a reminder that God cares about you? List some Scriptures below.**

# display

If you couldn't think of any promises of God to hold onto (or even if you could), spend some time looking for promises of God in the Bible today. A few verses you could look at are Philippians 4:6-7, Jeremiah 29:11, Matthew 11:28, John 3:16, or Joshua 1:9. Highlight a few of those verses in your Bible, and bookmark them for when you need reminders of the promises God has made to you.

God, thank You for keeping Your promises to Sarah, and reminding me that You keep Your promises to me, as well. Thank You for loving me so much that You take the time to care for me. Help me trust You each and every day of my life. Amen.

He took him outside and said, "Look at the sky and count the stars, if you are able to count them." Then he said to him, "Your offspring will be that numerous." Abram believed the LORD, and he credited it to him as righteousness.

—Genesis 15:5-6

# A COSTLY SACRIFICE

## discover

READ GENESIS 22:1-19.

**Then he said, "Do not lay a hand on the boy or do anything to him. For now I know that you fear God, since you have not withheld your only son from me."
—Genesis 22:12**

Think about what you treasure most in this world. Maybe it's a close family member or friend, or maybe it's something you worked for or waited a long period of time to get. Now think about how you would feel if you lost that item or relationship.

In Genesis 22, Abraham was faced with losing the thing he treasured the most; even more heartbreaking, he would lose it by his own hand. God had asked Abraham to sacrifice his son, Isaac, to Him. God was testing Abraham's faith, seeing if Abraham was willing to do anything to be obedient to Him. Abraham was. He followed God's instructions until the very last second. As the sacrificial knife was raised, God stopped Abraham and provided a better sacrifice so that Abraham and Isaac could worship God together.

God wants us to trust Him enough that we obey Him at all costs. Ultimately, God promises to provide what we need, so we can trust Him enough to give up everything we have. A reminder: God isn't going to ask you to do anything that He Himself isn't willing to do! How do we know? God provided a ram so that Isaac would be saved from death—a reminder of how God sacrificed His one and only Son on a cross so that we could be saved from eternal death.

# delight

**What do you consider your most treasured possession? Would you be willing to give it up for God?**

**From what we've read so far, why do you think Abraham trusted God with this difficult request?**

# display

Ask God to show you anything you are holding back from Him, or anything that is getting in the way of obeying Him fully. Sit in silence for five minutes as you ask God to reveal these obstacles to you. As He shows you things, write them down. When you are finished, think carefully about whether those things are more important than God. Pray that God would help you to treasure Him more than the things on your list.

**God, thank You for reminding me that You are most important in my life. Help me to remove anything that gets in the way of my relationship with You. Amen.**

# A BLIND DATE

## discover

READ GENESIS 24.

**Before he had finished speaking, there was Rebekah—
daughter of Bethuel son of Milcah, the wife of Abraham's
brother Nahor—coming with a jug on her shoulder.
—Genesis 24:15**

By Genesis 24, Abraham had gone from old to very old. He had received the promised son, Isaac, who had also grown up. It became time for Isaac to be married and have children of his own—which would have to happen for Abraham to continue his family tree and become the "father of many nations." Abraham sent one of his servants back to Abraham's relatives. He told his servant that there, God would provide a wife for Isaac. The servant followed Abraham's instructions and went back to his home and prayed to God; as soon as he finished, a beautiful young woman arrived right where the servant had stopped to water his camels. The entire encounter happened just as Abraham had said and just as the servant had prayed. That woman, Rebekah, would become Isaac's wife.

It would be easy for us if we were able to find the answer for every need we have on our own. However, that is not the reality for anyone. God didn't design us to be able to completely provide for ourselves. God wants us to trust Him to provide for our needs, whether physical, emotional, or spiritual. The good news for us is that God loves us. Because He loves us, He delights in providing for us, as a good Father does. Our response to His love is to pray to Him when there is something we need, and to wait patiently, trusting His provision and timing.

# delight

**Compare the servant's prayer to his encounter with Rebekah. How did the prayer line up with what happened?**

**What do these verses teach us about God? How can you apply these lessons about God to whatever circumstances you are facing today?**

# display

God provided for Isaac, as He provided for Abraham. How has He provided for you this week? Write down as many ways as you can think of (try to come up with at least ten).

**God, thank You for providing for me this week and each day. Thank You for being the perfect Father, one who provides for His children. Help me to never take for granted how You freely give. Please help me take my concerns to You whenever I have them. Thank You for always listening when I call. Amen.**

In The Beginning

# JACOB BECOMES ISRAEL

Selfish, manipulative, and not at all trustworthy—yep, I'm talking about Jacob. But as God changed Jacob's heart, He also changed his name. Jacob would become Israel, a man who wrestled with God and a beautiful illustration of God's transformative love.

# YOU AREN'T YOURSELF WHEN YOU'RE HUNGRY

## discover

READ GENESIS 25:19-34.

Jacob said, "Swear to me first." So he swore to Jacob and sold his birthright to him. Then Jacob gave bread and lentil stew to Esau; he ate, drank, got up, and went away. So Esau despised his birthright.
—Genesis 25:33-34

When the word "hangry" was added to the *Oxford English Dictionary* in 2015, it was thousands of years too late for Esau. However, I can't think of a better word to describe him! Esau and his twin brother, Jacob, were Isaac's sons. They couldn't have been more opposite: Esau was his father's favorite son and Jacob, his mother's. Esau was a skilled hunter who was always out in the open country and Jacob was a homebody. Most importantly, Esau—as first born over Jacob by mere seconds—was destined to receive extraordinary blessings from God, and Jacob, next to nothing.

At least, that was what was supposed to happen. After a long day of hunting, Esau returned home to the smell of Jacob's delicious homemade stew. Esau demanded some of it, but Jacob wanted to bargain. Jacob figured a meal this delicious was certainly worth Esau's birthright—the blessing given to the first-born son. Esau agreed, trading in his place as the eldest son and the double blessing that would have come with it.

Sometimes, in impatience or poor judgment, we exchange something of value for immediate satisfaction. This could mean compromising our morals for social acceptance, buying something we want (but don't need) before we can really afford it, or sacrificing our commitment to God for something less than eternal, here on earth. We should remember to cherish things that are lasting—and things God says are important—above all else.

# delight

Have you ever made a poor decision to give up something valuable for something else much less valuable? In that situation, what caused you to make such a poor choice?

Now that you've identified your weakness, ask God to help you battle against it so that you can treasure the things worth treasuring in the future. Write out your prayer to God below.

# display

Write a list of things that God wants you to treasure and prioritize. Make a commitment to God that you won't trade these relationships, values, or other possessions for lesser things.

**God, thank You for blessing me with treasures that You did not have to give me. Help me honor You by the way I care for my family, friends, possessions, body, and mind. Please give me the strength to guard these things above all else. Also, please renew, forgive, and restore me when I fall short. Amen.**

# DAY 18

# TWICE

## discover

READ GENESIS 27.

**Isaac began to tremble uncontrollably. "Who was it then," he said, "who hunted game and brought it to me? I ate it all before you came in, and I blessed him. Indeed, he will be blessed!"**
**—Genesis 27:33**

Unfortunately for Esau, his brother was not done taking advantage of him. When Isaac became old, he decided it was time to bestow his blessing on his sons. Although Esau had given up his birthright and his right to the "double blessing" that came with being the first-born, Isaac still had a blessing to give him. But Isaac had become near-blind in his old age, and Jacob and his mother decided to take advantage of his weak eyesight. When it came time for Esau to be blessed, Rebekah sent Jacob in to steal the blessing—equipped with fur to mimic Esau's hairy skin and the fresh food to copy Esau's hunting prowess. Isaac couldn't tell enough difference to avoid being tricked, and he blessed Jacob instead of Esau. By the time Esau arrived on the scene, it was too late. This led Esau into a furious rage and a desire to kill his brother.

Jacob was forced to leave his family and homeland to escape the wrath of his brother. Jacob's deception had cost him a lot. Anytime we seek to gain through cheating or other deceptive means, we will ultimately be the ones who lose. Jacob's scheming caused fighting between his descendants and Esau's descendants for generations. When we feel the temptation to try and get ahead by doing evil, we should be the ones who think twice.

# delight

**What negatives came as a result of Jacob's deception?**

**Have you ever tried to get ahead by dishonest means? What was the ultimate result?**

# display

We all have hurt the feelings of someone close to us, whether on purpose or through an honest mistake. Either way, we should seek to make amends any time we cause pain to someone around us. Think about the last time you treated someone close to you poorly. The next time you see them, admit your mistake and ask for forgiveness. Whenever we hurt someone, it is best to ask for forgiveness and seek to mend relationships as soon as possible.

God, I am sorry for hurting those around me. Help me to be characterized by patience and love. I know when I treat others poorly, You are not honored. Help me to remember that when I am relating with other people. Please give me the wisdom and patience to treat people as You would treat them. Amen.

# THE PROCESS OF PROGRESS

## discover

READ GENESIS 28.

"Look, I am with you and will watch over you wherever you
go. I will bring you back to this land, for I will not leave
you until I have done what I have promised you."
—Genesis 28:15

I once took a pottery course for fun. Near the end of the course, we were supposed to mold a clay bowl. It seemed simple enough to me; however, I didn't realize the painstaking process and precise handwork it takes to turn a lump of clay into anything vaguely resembling a bowl! Eventually, though, I was able to create something worthwhile.

In Genesis 28, Jacob set out in search of a wife. During his journey, he fell asleep at night and had a dream. During the dream, God blessed him, continuing the promise given to Isaac and Abraham. God also promised to always be with him. Despite Jacob's selfishness and trickery, God loved Jacob and promised to provide for him. At the end of the chapter, Jacob committed his life and belongings to God. Even though he wasn't perfect, Jacob was turning more and more towards God. Like I did with that lump of clay, God was molding Jacob into who He wanted him to be.

God promises to do the same with us when we turn over our lives to Him. We will never be perfect until we are in His presence—but as we are in process, we are made more and more like Him. As we begin to see how God sees, we realize there is nothing more beautiful than seeing the world and everyone in it through God's eyes.

# delight

**Go back and look at God's promise to Abraham in Genesis 12. How does God's promise to Abraham compare to the promise God made to Jacob?**

**In what areas of your life are you turning more toward God?**

**In what areas of your life are you running away from God?**

# display

Find a lump of clay, Play-Doh, or a similar moldable substance. Place it on your dresser or nightstand. When you look at it, be reminded that we are all works in progress. Practically, this means we should offer grace and forgiveness to other people, and we should celebrate growth in our own walk with Jesus.

God, thank You for working in my life and continuing to make me more like You. Help me to be patient with other people, and thank You for personally giving me grace. Please give me the strength to continue to grow closer to You. Amen.

# YOU REAP WHAT YOU SOW

## discover

READ GENESIS 29:1-30.

**When morning came, there was Leah! So he said to Laban, "What have you done to me? Wasn't it for Rachel that I worked for you? Why have you deceived me?"**
**—Genesis 29:25**

On his journey to find a wife, Jacob eventually reached where his father Isaac had instructed him to go. Isaac had told Jacob to marry someone from his homeland. So Jacob returned to his father's homeland, and he met a beautiful woman named Rachel. Jacob was so eager to marry Rachel that he told her father, Laban, he would work for seven years in order to marry her. To Jacob, the years seemed like days because he loved Rachel so much.

However, when it came time for Jacob and Rachel to marry, it was Laban who pulled a trick on Jacob! He brought his oldest daughter, Leah, to Jacob instead of doing as he agreed. In order for Jacob to also marry Rachel, Laban made him agree to work another seven years.

It is interesting that Jacob (an accomplished trickster) had the tables turned on him like this. In life we often find that we "reap what we sow." That means whatever we plant will grow until it is time for harvest. If we spread dishonesty, lies, or hostility, we will often find those returned to us, even if they don't come back until much later. But if we live with character and integrity, we will find people normally approach us in the same fashion. It is not the only reason we should treat others honestly, but Jacob's life is certainly a reminder of this principle.

# delight

**Write down examples from your life when you have "reaped what you have sown."**

**What did you learn from your situation?**

**Why is it important for us to treat other people fairly? Write down at least three different reasons.**

# display

Jacob worked seven years to marry Rachel, just to be tricked on his wedding day. However, in his life, he hadn't exactly been spreading honesty himself! This week, challenge yourself to give away seven dollars. It could be to your church as an offering, to a nonprofit or other organization, or to a person in need. Note: you do not have to do this, and you are not giving this money away in expectation of receiving anything back. However, unlike Jacob and Laban, God is a God of generosity. If you do choose to give the seven dollars, do so out of the generosity in your own heart, not to see if you can get anything back as a "reward" for your generosity.

**God, thank You for giving freely and openly. You are a generous God. Please help me to be generous as I seek to use my life to show others who You are. Help me to sow seeds of love, joy, and goodness wherever I go. Amen.**

# DAY 21

# TIME TO FACE THE MUSIC

## discover

READ GENESIS 32.

**"Your name will no longer be Jacob," he said. "It will be Israel because you have struggled with God and with men and have prevailed."**
**—Genesis 32:28**

Family dynamics are often complicated. If you asked Jacob about that, I'm fairly certain he would agree. As we continue to follow his story in Genesis, we see a few positives took place: Jacob's family continued to grow, and God continued to bless Jacob and all his possessions. Because of this, however, Jacob's father-in-law Laban and Laban's sons began to dislike Jacob. Jacob decided he had had enough and left to go back to his homeland. One problem: in order to go back home, he would have to encounter . . . (dramatic pause) his brother Esau.

On his way to face Esau, Jacob met a man and began to wrestle with him. Jacob would not release the man until he blessed Jacob. The man blessed Jacob and changed his name to Israel—because Jacob had struggled with man and God and prevailed. As you may have guessed, the man was no ordinary man: He was God. God again blessed Jacob—now called Israel—even though his life had been a struggle. Jacob would be the namesake of a new group of people, the Israelites. God was with Israel and God was for Israel, which meant he could make it through the struggles of life, even though they were difficult. No matter what you are going through, God promises to be with you too, and that promise will never cease. He will see you through.

# delight

**What struggles are you currently going through in your life?**

**Have you faced your struggles head-on, or are you trying to avoid dealing with them for as long as possible? Even though it is hard to deal with rough situations, God promises to be with you. Ask Him to help you deal with your struggles today.**

# display

Take time to pray over the struggles you wrote down. Make a plan to deal with the struggles you are going through, whether it is a relationship that needs mending, a sin issue that needs accountability, or an emotional scar you need to talk to someone about. Reach out to a trusted adult if you need help confronting this struggle.

**God, thank You for promising to be with me, even through the dark and difficult times. Help me to have the courage to face my struggles head-on. Please help me to feel Your presence and power in my life. Thank You for being my God. Amen.**

# DAY 22

# REUNITED (AND IT FEELS SO GOOD)

## discover

READ GENESIS 33.

**But Esau ran to meet him, hugged him, threw his arms around him, and kissed him. Then they wept.**
**—Genesis 33:4**

The time had come for the face off between Jacob and Esau. As Jacob and his family approached Canaan, they looked and saw Esau coming towards them . . . with 400 men. Gulp. But this family reunion was what no one could have expected. As Jacob bowed toward Esau, asking for forgiveness, Esau ran to his brother and hugged him closely. They cried together. Between the two, all was forgiven. They met each other's children—their own nieces and nephews—and Jacob settled with his family in Canaan. There, Jacob worshiped God as his Lord and God, and called Him "the God of Israel."

Jacob had a hard choice to make—stay with Laban or to face his brother and try to mend their relationship—but he did the right thing. The amazing thing is that God met Jacob in the hard moments as he did his best to make the wise choice. God will do the same for you. Jacob had seen God show up for him time and time again and developed his own faith and dependence on God. That is why Jacob could call Him "the God of Israel." We also must rely on God, individually and personally. Our parents, friends, and neighbors may or may not worship God as their own, but God wants a personal relationship specifically with us. We must trust Him with our hearts, minds, and lives so we can call Him our Father—our God.

# delight

**If you were in Esau's shoes, how would you have acted toward Jacob?**

**Read Ephesians 4:32. Why does God say we should be quick to forgive?**

# display

In the previous day's devotion, you made a plan to face your struggles head-on. Have you followed through with that plan? If you have, how did it go? If you have not, what is holding you back?

Below, write down the names of some people who you need to forgive, and pray for God to bless them.

**God, thank You for being the God who brings people to Himself. I know You want us to reconcile with other people, too. Help me to see who I need to forgive, and please give me the strength to forgive them. Thank You for forgiving me for the things I have done wrong. Thank You for loving me, no matter what. Amen.**

# JOSEPH
## AND THE
## SOVEREIGNTY
## OF GOD

Joseph trusted God despite his circumstances—and some of them were unbelievable circumstances! Joseph's dependence on God set the stage for God's biggest plot twist yet, and his life shows we can trust God, no matter what.

# DAY 23

# JEALOUS EYES

## discover

READ GENESIS 37.

**"So now, come on, let's kill him and throw him into one of the pits. We can say that a vicious animal ate him. Then we'll see what becomes of his dreams!"**
**—Genesis 37:20**

Jealousy is a dangerous thing. At its core, jealousy occurs when we are so ungrateful for what we have that we strongly desire something belonging to someone else. Jealousy is dangerous because it not only causes us to feel negatively about ourselves or our circumstances; it also causes us to feel negatively about someone else. Often, jealousy compels us to make bad choices.

Joseph was an object of jealousy for his brothers. After all, he was very clearly Jacob's favorite son. You could argue his brothers' jealousy was partly his fault—he spoke openly about having a dream where his brothers bowed down and worshiped him. But Joseph did not deserve what happened to him next. His brothers were so jealous of him, and hated him so much, that they decided to kill him. When Joseph's oldest brother, Rueben, vetoed that idea, they decided instead to sell him into slavery. They took Joseph's robe, tore it up, and stained it with blood, leading Jacob to believe his favorite son had been mauled by a wild beast; their father's heart was broken to pieces. Despite this wickedness, God was orchestrating a story that would change the course of history. As Joseph himself would later say: "You planned evil against me; God planned it for good" (Gen. 50:20).

# delight

**When was a time you became jealous of someone else? What caused your jealousy?**

**In the situation you wrote about above, how could you have counteracted your jealousy? What blessing from God can you thank Him for instead of becoming jealous in another similar situation?**

# display

Write down ten things that you are thankful for. When you are tempted to become jealous of someone else, remember that comparison is the thief of joy! God has you placed exactly where you are supposed to be. When you need it, look at your list here to remember how much God has blessed you.

**God, thank You for providing for me in ways more than I can count. Help me to have a heart of thankfulness, not one of jealousy. Help me to be confident in where You have placed me, and help me to honor You well in how I live each moment. Amen.**

# NOT ALONE

## discover

READ GENESIS 39.

**Although she spoke to Joseph day after day,
he refused to go to bed with her.
—Genesis 39:10**

For humans, one of the worst feelings is loneliness. The idea of being alone with no one around to care about you—it's a terrifying thought. I imagine that's how Joseph felt: sold into slavery on a caravan of strangers, headed to an unknown destination . . ."lonely" probably doesn't even begin to describe his state of mind.

But Joseph was not alone. He had with him exactly who he needed: God. Joseph was bought by Potiphar, a royal official of the Egyptian king, Pharaoh. Potiphar recognized God was with Joseph and placed Joseph in charge of his entire household. Joseph had great success in Egypt because God was with him.

That is, until Potiphar's wife tried to tempt Joseph into sin. Joseph rejected her advances, so Potiphar's wife framed him. As an outsider, Joseph stood no chance against these accusations and was wrongfully thrown in jail. The good news for Joseph: no one can thwart God's plans. Even in jail, God granted Joseph favor with those around him. God was with him—and the reminder for us is that even when we feel alone, we should remember that God is always with us, too.

# delight

**Go back and re-read chapter 39. How many times are we reminded that God was with Joseph?**

**In your life, when have you most felt like you were alone?**

**How does remembering that God is with you encourage you today?**

# display

Take a stack of sticky notes and write "You are not alone. – Genesis 39:21" on each of them. Ask God where you should place them—on the lockers near yours at school, at your local coffee shop, around your house, on car windshields at the grocery store, or in another location. Use these sticky notes to remind yourself and others of God's presence.

**God, thank You for always being with me. Please remind me of this when I feel alone. Amen.**

# MEMORY VERSE

You planned evil against me; God planned it for good to bring about the present result—the survival of many people.

—Genesis 50:20

## DAY 25

# FORGET ME NOT

## discover

READ GENESIS 40.

**"We had dreams," they said to him, "but
there is no one to interpret them."
Then Joseph said to them, "Don't interpretations
belong to God? Tell me your dreams."
—Genesis 40:8**

Just when Joseph though his situation couldn't get any worse, he was thrown into prison for a crime he didn't commit. Ouch! But even in prison, God continued to do amazing things in Joseph's life. The captain of the jail liked him and put him in charge. Eventually two important people were tossed in prison, as well—Pharaoh's cup-bearer and his baker.

Both the cup-bearer and the baker had interesting dreams while they were in prison, but neither of them knew what these dreams meant. Joseph suggested they should tell their dreams to him. They did, and Joseph interpreted the dreams for them—two dreams with very different outcomes. God revealed the meaning of the dreams to Joseph and both dreams came true exactly as Joseph said they would. The cup-bearer, whose dream meant he would be reinstated to his position in Pharaoh's palace, said that he would remember Joseph. But he didn't, leaving Joseph to remain in prison.

Although the cup-bearer forgot about Joseph, God never did. As we will soon see, God was thinking of Joseph the whole time. The same is true for us: God will never forget about us. He doesn't even need to remember us. He is always thinking of us, writing a plan for His glory and our good in our lives. Even when it doesn't feel like it, God is making a way for us—just as He was for Joseph.

# delight

**Joseph could have grown bitter about his circumstances, but he didn't. How do you stay faithful, even when the circumstances of your life are challenging?**

**God was working even while Joseph was suffering in prison. When has there been a time in your life when you later realized God was working in the midst of suffering?**

# display

In the Psalms, a constant theme is the idea of remembering. The authors of the Psalms often asked God to remember them, knowing He would because He is faithful. Write your own short psalm to God. Start by asking Him to remember you, and then write out the characteristics of God that remind you why He would never forget you (feel free to look at a few of the Psalms for inspiration).

**God, thank You for never forgetting about me. You are faithful and kind. You love abundantly. Thank You for writing a plan for my life. Please remember me when things seem to be going against me. Help me to trust You when I feel discouraged. Amen.**

# DAY 26

# PROMOTION

## discover

READ GENESIS 41.

**So Pharaoh said to Joseph, "Since God has made all this known to you, there is no one as discerning and wise as you are. You will be over my house, and all my people will obey your commands. Only I, as king, will be greater than you." Pharaoh also said to Joseph, "See, I am placing you over all the land of Egypt."**
**—Genesis 41:39-41**

Déjà vu is the feeling that you have experienced something before, especially through a dream. When we read that Pharaoh himself had a couple of dreams he didn't understand, we might get a feeling of biblical déjà vu! Thankfully, the cup-bearer finally remembered that he left poor Joseph sitting in prison, and Pharaoh called on Joseph to use his God-given ability to interpret dreams. Joseph explained that a famine was coming which would devastate the land. Joseph even proposed a solution. Pharaoh recognized God's wisdom in Joseph, and appointed him second-in-command over all of Egypt. Talk about a promotion!

Sold into slavery. Falsely accused. Jailed. Forgotten. These were all part of God's plan. Even though Joseph couldn't see it at the time, God was perfectly constructing a beautiful story of Joseph's elevation to being one of the most powerful men in the world. At times, you probably have questions about what God is doing with your story as well. God sees you. He loves you—no matter what. As you study His Word, recognize that God wants you to trust Him and to see how He proves Himself over and over again. It will probably take patience and waiting, but God is crafting your story, too. Like Joseph, you can trust your life in God's hands.

# delight

**Joseph exercised great patience waiting on God's plan to come together. How do you exercise patience in your life for God's plan to come together?**

**Which elements of Joseph's story encourage you the most?**

# display

Find a jigsaw puzzle in your house or a digital jigsaw puzzle on the internet. First, try to solve the puzzle without looking at the image that shows the finished picture. This is often what our life looks like to us. Then, solve the puzzle using the master image. This is what our life looks like to God, because He can see the entire story! Remember this whenever you feel discouraged or confused by your circumstances. If you can, keep a piece of the puzzle (or a picture of a puzzle piece) in your pocket or close by to remind you of this truth—just remember to put it back later!

**God, thank You for being in control of everything. Please forgive me for the times when I questioned You or had doubts about Your plan. Please remind me of Your goodness and power when I need to be reminded. Help me to trust You every day. Amen.**

# DAY 27

# FULL CIRCLE

## discover

READ GENESIS 42.

**The sons of Israel were among those who came to buy grain, for the famine was in the land of Canaan. Joseph was in charge of the country; he sold grain to all its people. His brothers came and bowed down before him with their faces to the ground.**
**—Genesis 42:5-6**

Seven years of plenty, followed by seven years of famine. It happened exactly as God had spoken through Joseph. During those years of plenty, Joseph organized the storage of so much grain that they could not measure it all. Pharaoh ordered that anyone who needed to eat would have to come see Joseph. Through Joseph, Egypt would be saved.

And, as it turns out, more than just Egypt! The famine had spread . . . well, basically everywhere. People from all over had heard that there was grain in Egypt and began to travel there to buy food. This included the land of Canaan, where Joseph's family lived. Jacob, still living but old, sent his sons to Egypt. They came into Joseph's presence, and bowed before who they thought was an Egyptian official. Joseph's dream from many years earlier had come true (see Gen. 37:5-7)—but Joseph's brothers didn't recognize him! Joseph had a decision to make: What would happen next?

In God's plan, things often work out in a way we never expect. Situations some see as coincidence are often purposeful movements made by God to remind us of His presence and power. Whether things look like chaos or are extraordinary organized, remember these truths—God is in charge, He has a plan, and we can trust Him, no matter what.

# delight

**In what areas of your life is it hardest for you to trust God?**

**Do you typically rely on God's wisdom or your own wisdom? Why?**

# display

At the top of this page in your Bible, write "God's Timing > Our Timing." If you have a group chat with friends, take a picture of that page and send it in your group chat. Encourage those around you (and yourself) that waiting for God's timing is always the best idea.

**God, thank You for Your perfect wisdom. Help me to patiently wait on You to work and move in my life. Please forgive me for the times when I try to make things happen on my own. Please guide me and show me Your plan, in Your timing. Amen.**

# DAY 28

# REVENGE?

## discover

READ GENESIS 45.

**Then Joseph said to his brothers, "Please, come near me," and they came near. "I am Joseph, your brother," he said, "the one you sold into Egypt. And now don't be grieved or angry with yourselves for selling me here, because God sent me ahead of you to preserve life."**
**—Genesis 45:4-5**

Ever had the temptation to take revenge on someone who did you wrong? I suspect we all have had that temptation. Check out Joseph in Genesis 45. Talk about an opportunity for revenge! In front of him: his brothers bowed, asking for the food they need to survive. In his hands: the choice to give them what the needed or not—essentially their very lives. In his heart and mind: the hurt and pain they caused him all those years before. Definitely movie-level drama.

Of all the options Joseph had, he ultimately chose forgiveness. He left behind the years of struggle and any feelings of resentment, and he provided for his brothers. Even more than just giving them the grain they needed, he provided them a new place to live and gave them more than they could have ever imagined. Joseph's viewpoint was that God had taken care of him this whole time specifically for this moment: so that he could rescue his family when they needed him. God had provided for him, so he would provide for them.

In a moment when he could have hurt his brothers for their mistreatment of him, Joseph saw things how God saw them. Even when people treat us unfairly, we should submit to God and seek to do things His way— especially when we are tempted to take revenge.

# delight

**How does it challenge you to know that Joseph forgave his brothers when he had the power to get revenge?**

**Why is it important to see things through God's perspective, instead of simply relying on our own understanding?**

# display

God used Joseph to provide for his family and others around him. How can you help provide for someone around you? Below, think about some people around you who may need help. Write down a way you can help solve their need, and make a plan to follow through this week.

God, help me to forgive those around me who have caused me hurt. Thank You for providing everything I need, including making a way for me to be forgiven when I sin. Please help me to care for others the way You care about me. Please give me the strength and wisdom to live that out with my actions. Amen.

# RE-ROUTING

## discover

READ GENESIS 46:1-7,28-34.

God said, "I am God, the God of your father. Do not be afraid
to go down to Egypt, for I will make you into a great nation
there. I will go down with you to Egypt, and I will also bring
you back. Joseph will close your eyes when you die."
—Genesis 46:3-4

When I was in 4th grade, my parents made the decision to move our family across the country to a new home. God had told them it was time to move—and although we were leaving behind the family and friends I had lived around my entire life, I remember my parents being confident because they knew they were being obedient. It would bring the unknown into our lives because it was a new experience, but they were sure God would provide everything we needed.

In Genesis 46, God told Jacob to take his family to Egypt. It was a foreign land away from his home, and Jacob could have been stubborn or afraid. But he chose to trust God, who had provided for his grandfather Abraham and his father Isaac. Jacob had seen God's faithfulness in his life, too. So Jacob obeyed. In Egypt, Jacob's family would grow to more than a million people. Through those people, God would change the world, and in Egypt, God would do one of His most incredible works. Because Jacob trusted God, his people would be part of something that would last forever: God's story of how He made a way for the whole world to be rescued.

# delight

**What's scary about trying something new or experiencing change?**

**From what you have seen so far in Genesis, what happens when we obey God?**

**In your own words, what does it mean to have faith? Why is having faith difficult? Why is having faith important?**

# display

Below, write five commitments you want to make to God. Tell Him when and why you will follow Him (e.g., I will obey you God, even when I don't know where You are leading). Take a picture of your list of commitments and set it as your phone background so that you will see it and remember daily.

**God, thank You for being Jehovah-Jireh, the perfect Provider. Please help me to remember that You give abundantly more than I could even ask for. Please help me to remember that You provide through perfect methods and in perfect timing. Please help me to have the courage to follow You in all situations. Amen.**

# DAY 30

# TRUST AND OBEY

## discover

READ GENESIS 50.

**"You planned evil against me; God planned it for good to bring about the present result—the survival of many people."**
**—Genesis 50:20**

Throughout Genesis we see a recurring idea: God is in control, and those that trust Him and follow His plan are blessed. Even when we cannot understand what God is doing, we can rest in knowing that He knows and He doesn't make mistakes. Our job is to trust and obey, even when those around us say differently.

Even though Noah had no concept of a flood, he built the ark. Even when Abraham was old, he trusted that God would give him a son so that he could become "the father of many." Even though Sarah laughed, she honored God when He gave her Isaac. Isaac saw God provide a ram for the sacrifice so that he could live, and Isaac trusted God and passed God's blessing onto Jacob. Jacob learned to trust God despite his trickster personality, and worshiped God as his personal God. And Joseph trusted God through years of loneliness, praising God that his personal struggle resulted in the rescue of his family. He didn't pay back evil when he had the chance, recognizing God's hand in his life the entire time.

Each of these people had faith that God would do what He promised. All are a part of God's story, and although they didn't see the entire story for themselves, you have seen their stories. God's invitation to them is the same one He gives to you: Will you trust Him and obey Him?

# delight

**To you, what has been the most memorable example of God's plan coming together in the book of Genesis? Why does this example stand out to you?**

**How has this book encouraged and grown your trust in God?**

# display

Go back to the memory verse on pages 90–91. This memorable quote was spoken by Joseph. Take some time to re-read and think about everything it meant for him to say these words. Work on committing this passage to memory so that you have it solidly in your heart for when you need it. Recall this verse whenever something comes along in your life that is hard or challenging. God can use that situation for His glory and your good. Trust Him, obey, and see where He will take you and how He will use you through your trust and obedience to Him.

God, thank You for writing this beautiful story of how You take care of Your people. Please help me remember that You will take care of me in the same way. Please give me the strength to trust You and the power to obey You in my life. Thank You for loving me, and help me to love You more and more each day. Amen.

# Created for More

God called everything He created "good," and we're a part of that. But we were created to do far more than just exist; we were created for relationships with God and others, to take care of the rest of God's creation, and to glorify God in living out His good design.

## Created for Community

**Read Genesis 1:26; 2:18.**

You've probably heard the word "community" tossed around a lot—it can refer to the immediate geographic area you live in, to the people closest to you in proximity, or to other Christians you know and with whom you live out God's plan each day. God Himself has built-in community between the Father, Son, and Holy Spirit. So when He created us in His image, He meant for us to have close relationships with Him and with other Christians.

**How often do you seek Jesus by spending time in prayer or God's Word on your own (outside of church)?**

| 1 | 2 | 3 | 4 | 5 |
|---|---|---|---|---|
| Never. | | When I have time. | | Every day! |

**How important is it to you that your closest friends are also seeking Jesus?**

| 1 | 2 | 3 | 4 | 5 |
|---|---|---|---|---|
| I don't really think about it. | | Sort of. | | 100 percent. |

**How much would you say others opinions affect the types of friends you pursue. (Fill in the bar).**

| 0% | 50% | 100% |
|---|---|---|

**Do you wish any of these numbers would change? What steps can you take to change them this week?**

# Created for Care

**Read Genesis 1:26b,28.**

Depending on which Scripture translation you read, you'll see words like "rule," "dominion over," or "reign over." The point is the same for all of these: we were created to "work . . . and watch over" the earth (Gen. 2:15). You don't have to be an environmental activist to care for God's creation. You can watch over it right where He has you.

**Here are some ideas. Check the one(s) you'd like to do most.**

_____ 1. Participate in an ocean, river, creek, or lake cleanup. (Or, if you happen to be on the water, take a trash bag, pick up any trash you see, and take it to be recycled or thrown away later.)

_____ 2. Be aware of things like "Leave No Trace," when hiking or exploring the outdoors. Basically, make sure you walk out with whatever you bring in.

_____ 3. Gather some friends or work with a club at school to clean up a sports stadium or field after weekly games.

_____ 4. Create a small garden in your backyard.

Consider choosing one idea (or coming up with your own!) and finding a way to do it in your community, then check with your parents to make sure you act safely.


# Created for His Glory

**Read Genesis 2:15-17; 3; Matthew 5:16; 1 Corinthians 10:31.**

We were created to make God's name great—or glorify Him—but from the beginning of time, people have wanted to make a name for themselves, instead. We make God's name great by acknowledging who He is in all that we do—in other words, through obedience to His commands.

**List two ways you can glorify God today.**

# LIFEWAY STUDENT DEVOTIONS
## Engage with God's Word.

lifeway.com/teendevotionals

☐ **THE COME BACK**

☐ **JESUS 101**

☐ **FUELED**

☐ **ALREADY BUT NOT YET**

☐ **THE ESSENTIALS**

☐ **CALLED**

☐ **PRESENCE & PURPOSE**

☐ **REVEALED**

☐ **LION OF JUDAH**

☐ **YOUR WILL BE DONE**

☐ **SPIRIT & TRUTH**

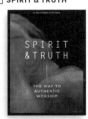

☐ **THREE-IN-ONE**